The Christmas 1
Delights

Karen Lord and Shanée Buxton

Follow us on Facebook @creativechameleonbooks
creativechameleonbooks@gmail.com

Also by Creative Chameleon Books

Anxious Armadillo
Gorgeous George
Cranky Crab
Theodore James Harrison Brown
I'm Better Than You
Hey, Dragonfly!

ISBN 978-1-914408-88-5

Dedicated to all children at Christmas.

Thank you for your inspiration
Loulla x

McKenna and Araya
Karen

It was the week before Christmas and the house on the hill,
Stood in darkness, quiet and still.
While the family were snuggled all cosy in beds...

...up in the loft above their heads,
Old furniture was stacked high and dusty,
A cradle, some old toys all cobwebbed and musty.

And tucked in the corner, all tatty and brown,
Stood a cardboard box....
    ...which quivered and jiggled up and down.

It started shaking, shuddering and shifting,
The flap on the box was slowly lifting.

"They've forgotten us!" came a voice from inside.

"Maybe they don't want us!" another voice cried.

"Don't be so silly, they need me on their tree!"

"But you're not as important as little old me!"

"We're always the first the family takes out!"

"But no one has fetched us," a little voice shouts.

"We need to get out and remind them we're here!"

From inside the box, there came a big cheer!

Hurrah!

The flap lifted up...

...out rolled the baubles, shiny and red.

Out waddled the penguins with a hat on their head.

Out danced the fairies, elegant and tall.

Out marched the soldiers who saluted them all.

Out fluttered the tinsel, gaudy and brash.

Out popped some snowmen with noses that flash.

Out came the lights tangled and twisted,

"They won't forget us!" the lights insisted.

"We're first on the tree, every year!"

"We're so much brighter than anyone here!"

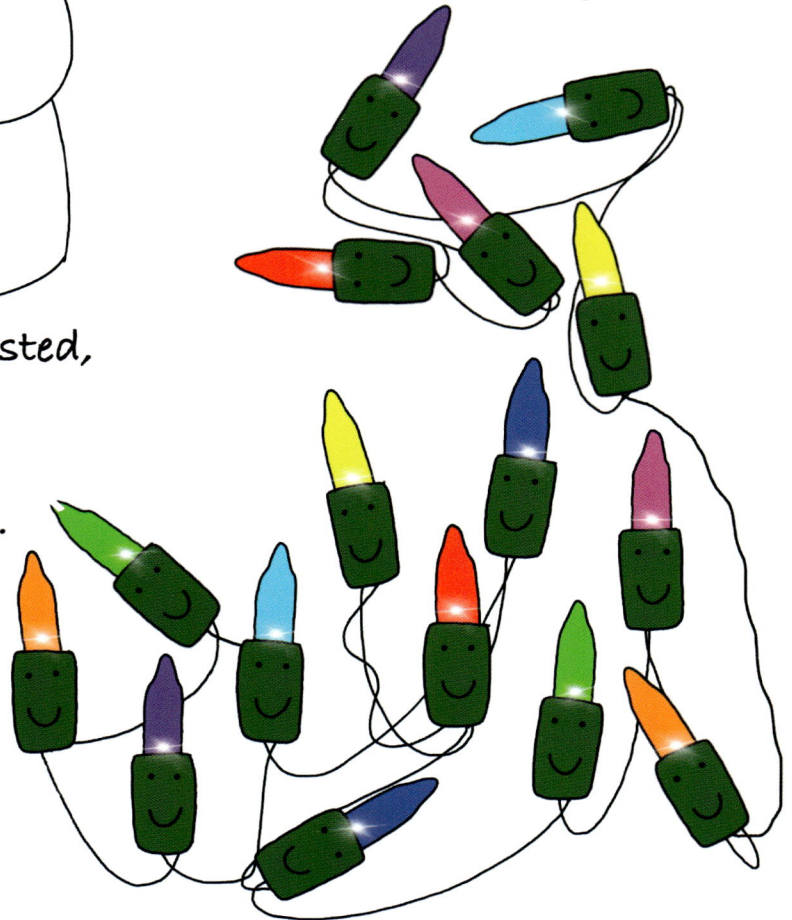

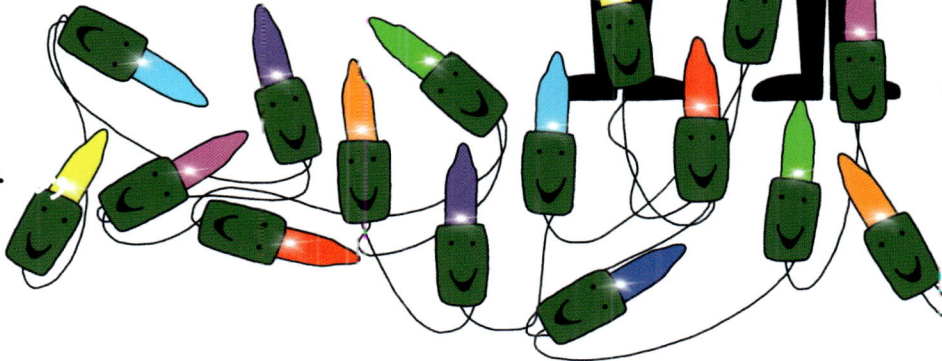

Then out of the box, sparkly and bright,
A star appeared and said with delight,

"Please don't argue, please don't shout,
This is not what Christmas is about!"

A fairy stepped forward...

"You're just one little star, who sits at the top of the tree,
There are lots of us here who are more important, can't you see?"

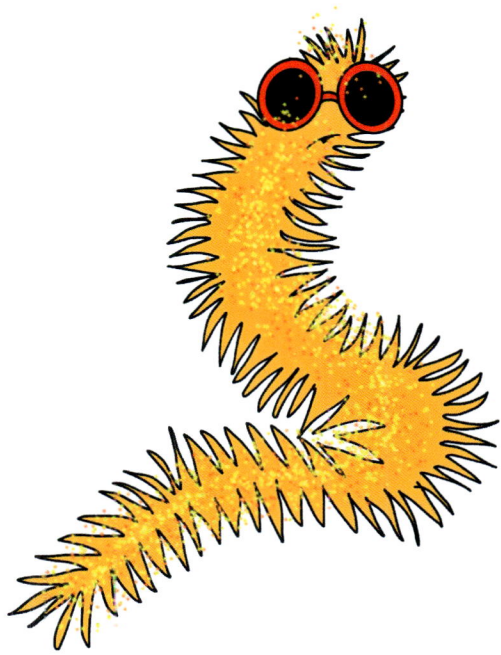

"The family need us, we make Christmas the best!"

"You're not better than us! Give it a rest!"

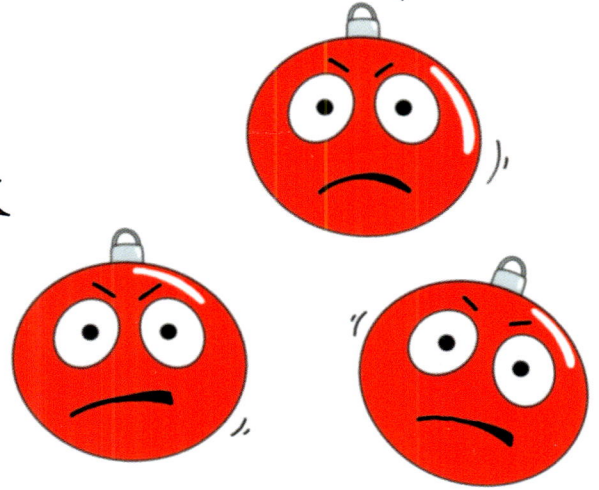

A penguin flapped his wings...

"Let's show the star what we can do!
This Christmas contest is way over due!"

Yes!

Yes!

Yes!

Yes!

Yes, that's true!

The lights untangled, plug hit the socket,
They flashed and twinkled and lit up like a rocket.
They danced in a circle, twisting and spinning,
Until they were all tangled, like in the beginning.

Star watched...

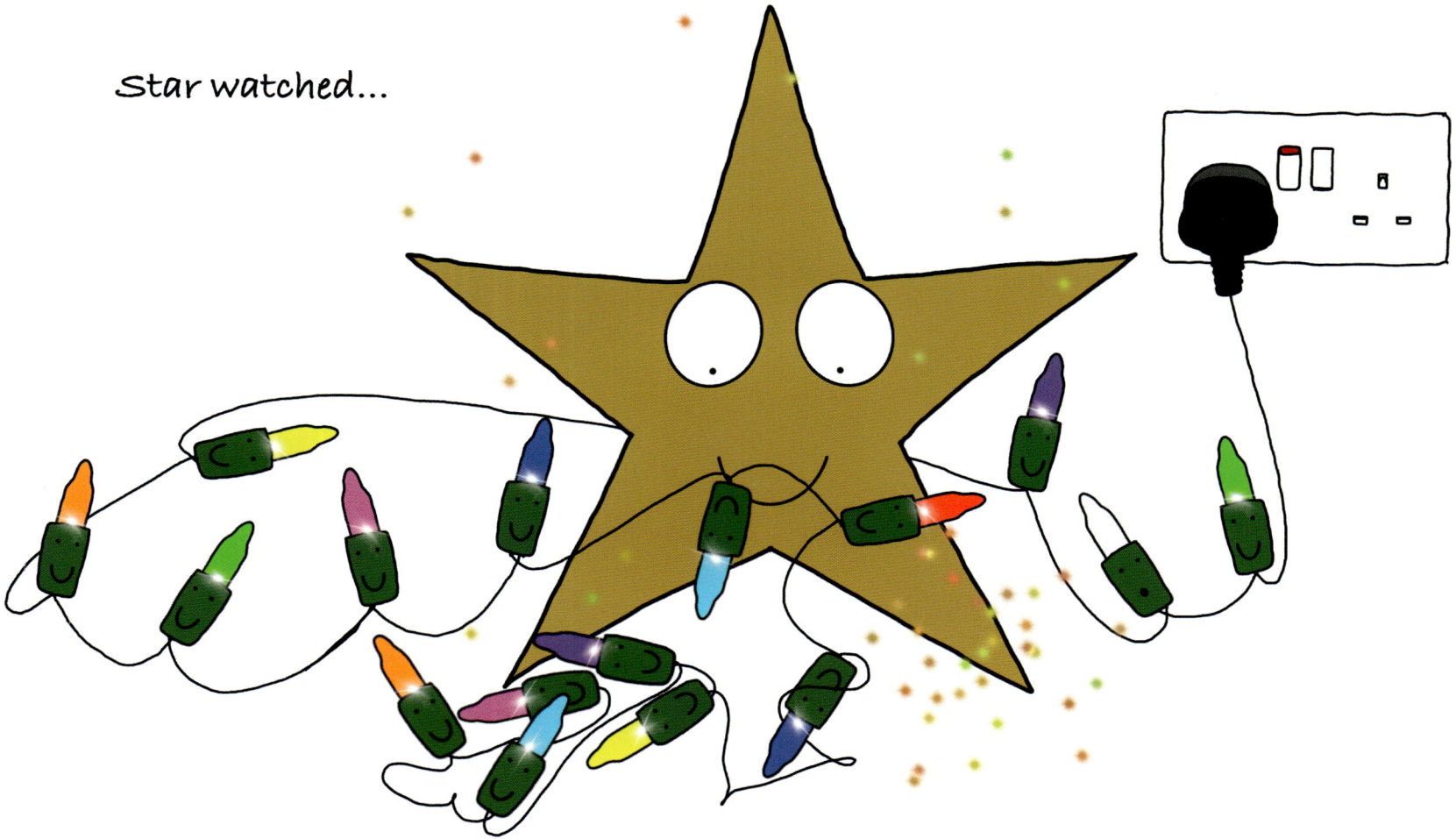

"You really are quite lovely, but look, he's gone out,
I'm sorry, fairy lights are not what Christmas is about!"

The tinsel giggled nervously…

"We're pretty, witty and very bright.
Star, watch us! We know we are just right!"

They shook their strips from side to side lightly,
And shimmered like snowflakes gleaming brightly.

Star smiled…

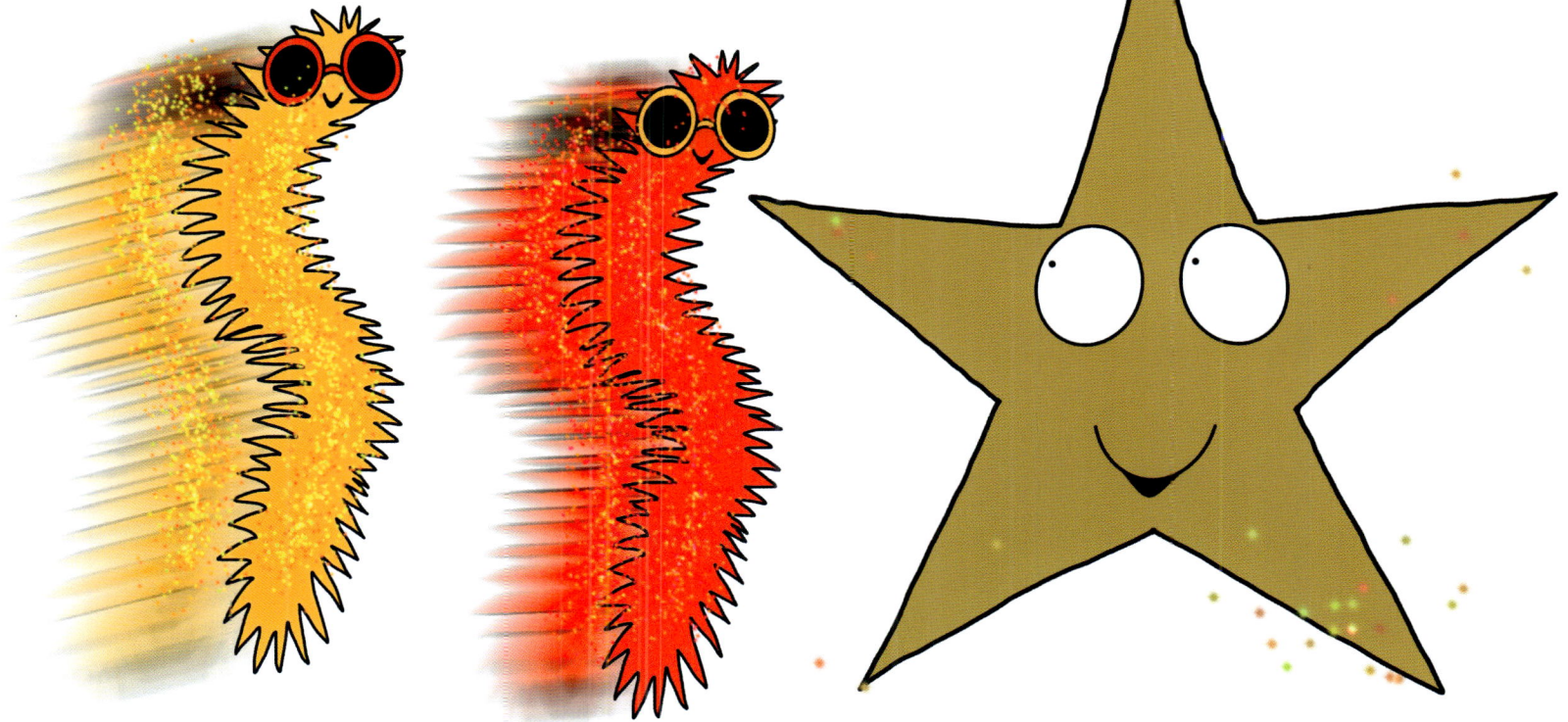

"You really are quite charming, that is without a doubt,
But sorry, sparkly tinsel is not what Christmas is about!"

The faries pirouetted over to the star...

"We're so important on the tree!

We're beautiful and elegant,
just you watch and see!"

The faries did a grand-jete and landed softly on their toes,
"We're the best!" they shouted, "Everybody knows!"

Star beamed...

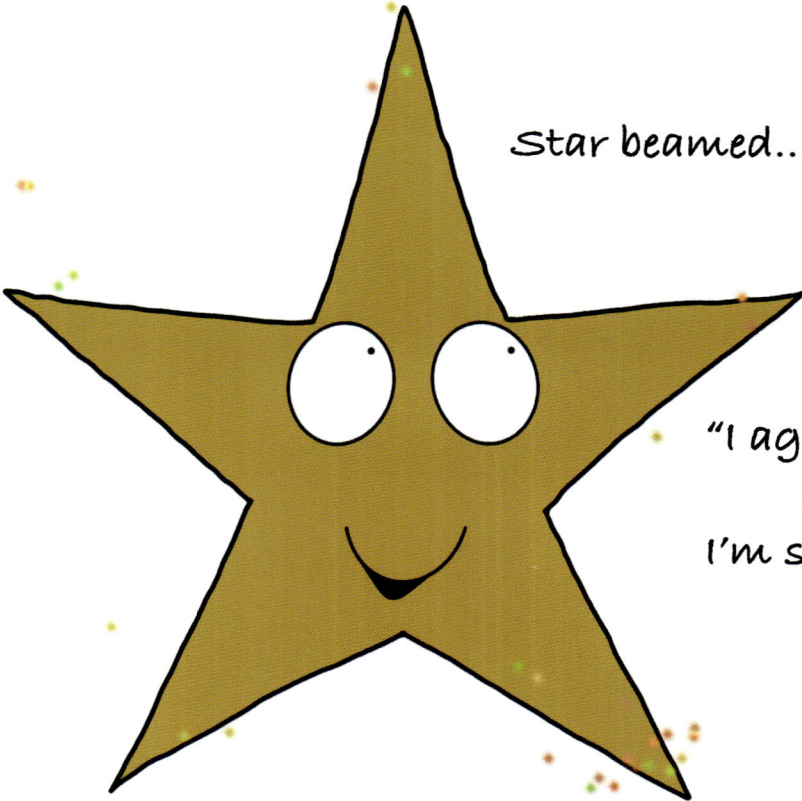

"I agree, you are beautiful and elegant,
and there is no need to shout!
I'm sorry, dancing fairies is not what
Christmas is about!"

The shiny red baubles rolled across towards the star.

"We're the most important decorations here by far.
We're round and very delicate, in our glory we hang on the tree.
We are just like little mirrors, reflecting what we see."

Star grinned...

"Baubles, you are very pretty,
        and good at what you do.
But I'm sorry to tell you all,
        there's more to Christmas than you!"

LEFT, RIGHT, LEFT, RIGHT. ATTENTION!
The soldiers all marched forward and stood in a straight line,
Black hats tall, red suits stylish and looking very fine.

"We are the Queen's soldiers and so MUST be the best!
We march in time and look smart, a cut above the rest!"

Star shook his head...

"I can see you're smart and clever,
        and you do look good on the tree...

...but the Queen's marching soldiers are not what Christmas is, you'll see!"

The snowmen tottered forward and held hands in rows,
"Everyone needs a snowman, especially when it snows.
We brighten up the tree with our scarves and bobble hats,
Our colourful big buttons and tummies round and fat!"

Star shook his head slowly...

"I agree snow is really fun,
but not when the sun comes out!

I'm sorry, smiling snowmen are not what Christmas is about!"

The penguins looked at each other and whispered in a huddle,
One penguin turned around and said,
"Star, this really is a muddle!
    If Christmas is not about baubles...

..tinsel...

...or lights,

soldiers...

...fairies...

....or snowmen...

...then please put us right!"

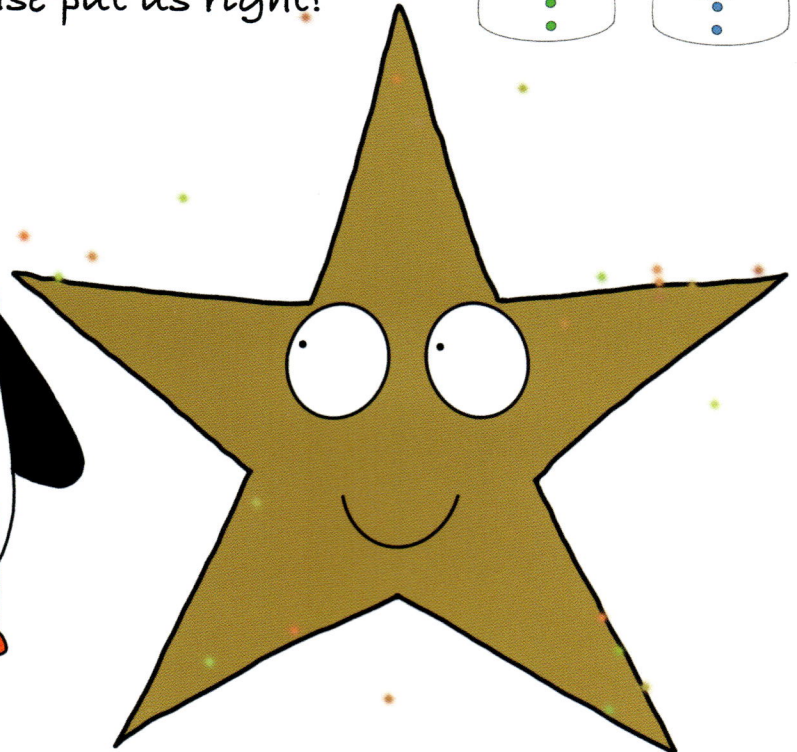

"Penguins always make people smile and never make a fuss,
So, if Christmas is not about the others, it must be about US!"

Star chuckled and patted the penguin...

"I love the way you wibble, all wobbly and stout,
Sorry guys, but you are not what Christmas is about!"

Star looked at all the decorations and puffed out his chest,
"This should not be a contest to find out who's the best.
I want you all to watch and see what Christmas is to me,
And why I am always put at the top of the tree."

The decorations gathered quietly under a dusty table,
As the star lifted up a red sheet, to reveal a wooden stable.

An innkeeper held up a lantern, shining clear and bright,
And all the decorations gasped at the truly wonderous sight.

Standing together, Mary and Joseph both looked down,
At a baby lying in a manger on hay of golden brown.
Shepherds and angels stood close by, and bowed to worship Him,
And nearby holding gifts, stood the three majestic Kings.

Star looked at the nativity...

"Look, Christmas is so much more!
It's not about tree decorations, or a wreath on the door.
You do add to the beauty of Christmas and bring the family joy,
But Christmas is all about the birth of this baby boy."

"We must never forget the true meaning of this special day,
As we celebrate Jesus' birthday on Christmas Day."

The decorations nodded...

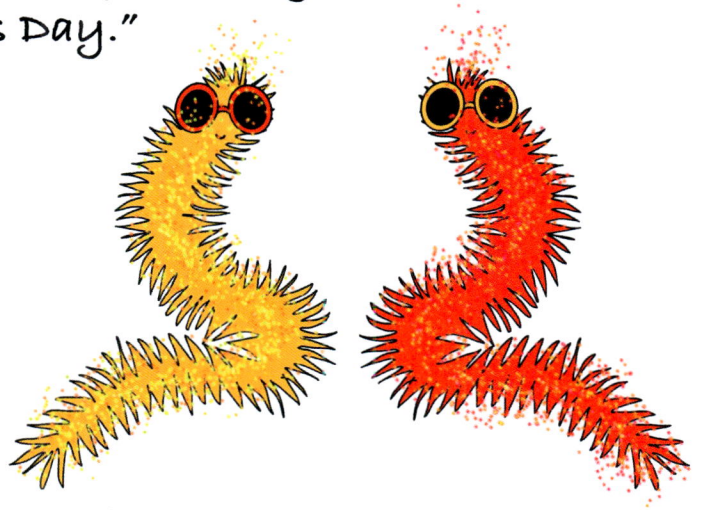

"We know we are pretty on the tree,
And we now understand that Christmas is not about me...

...or me!

...or me!

...or me!

...or me!

...or me!

...or me!"

It was the night before Christmas and the house on the hill,
Was lit up with excitement, not quiet and still.

Up in the loft, stacked high and dusty,
Was a cradle and furniture, all cobwebbed and musty.

And right in the corner,
all tatty and brown,
Was a cardboard box...
...patiently waiting to be taken down.

Suddenly, there was a creak and a small glint so bright,
As the loft door lifted and let in some light,

"They're coming for us!" whispered a voice from inside.

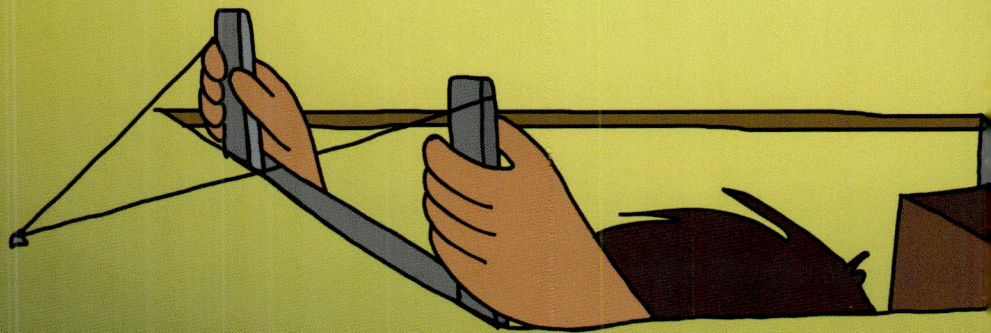

"I knew they would!" another voice cried.

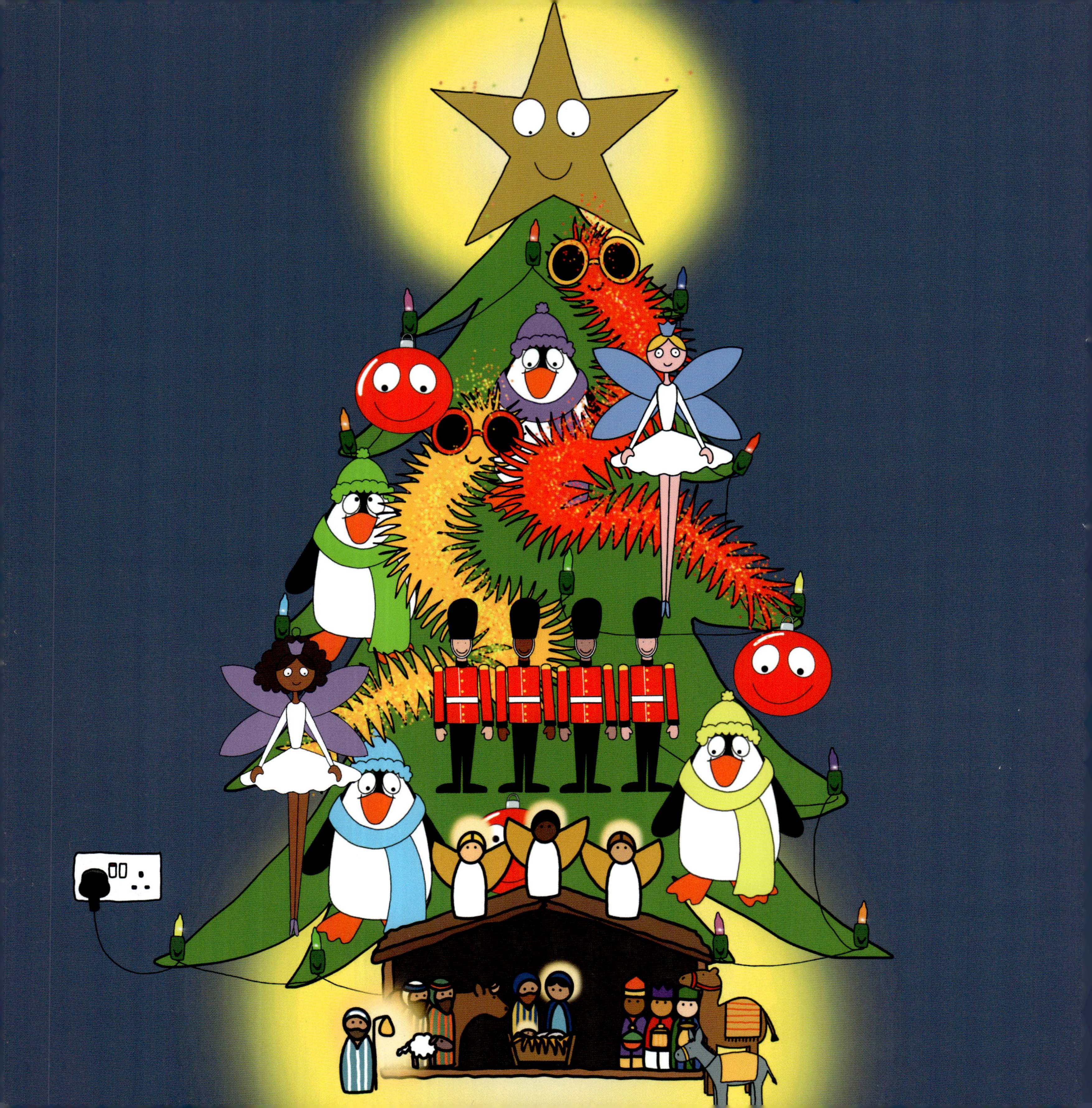

A very
Happy Christmas,
to everyone!